Praise for *Moving B*

"*Moving Beyond* is a devotional book specifically designed for anyone traveling through a valley. Millicent Flake combines stories from the Bible, her personal life experiences, and poignant questions to encourage and challenge the reader to faithfully walk through their valley, moving *beyond* it with God's love, grace, and forgiveness. Flake's scriptural knowledge combined with excellent questions draw the reader into stories with a fresh perspective. Each personal story fits like a glove with the theme and Bible character. I recommend this to anyone going through a difficult season."

— Dr. Jonathan Barlow

Senior Pastor, First Baptist Church, Dalton, Georgia

"In reading *Moving Beyond*, one experiences the rare opportunity of getting to know biblical persons in profoundly personal ways. Millicent Flake pulls back a curtain to reveal those we meet in scripture in a manner that objectively informs but, more profoundly, encourages authentic empathy. Relating to biblical figures in the flesh opens avenues for self-examination and life application. This bifold approach makes the book perfect for group study as well as individual spiritual growth."

— Mera Cossey Corlett, M.Div.

Senior Pastor, Okolona Baptist Church, Louisville, Kentucky

Moving Beyond

Journeying Through Life's Changes

Millicent Flake

Moving Beyond: Journeying Through Life's Changes

Millicent Flake, M. Div.

Published by Harbour Road Publishing
ISBN 978-1-387-69416-7

Cover art by Grey Von Cannon
www.greyvoncannon.com

Acknowledgements

Bringing this devotional book to reality has been a labor of love and prayer. Special thanks to everyone who has supported me on this journey.

To Amber Nagle, Vickie McEntire, and Rachel Kirkland for your feedback and technical skills and for always being my cheerleaders!

To Jonathan Barlow and Mera Corlett for your encouragement and early readings.

And especially to Keith for understanding when I close the door and tap away on the computer for hours at a time. Thank you for being the wind beneath my sails.

Contents

Moving Beyond
Journeying Through Life's Changes

Introduction

Introduction

Change is exhausting.

When I retired from my career as a school media specialist in 2019, I was not prepared for the emotional roller coaster I experienced. I went from euphoria over being freed from the responsibilities and constriction of working full time to deep sadness over leaving the people and routine that I had loved for many years. Transitioning to my new way of life was more challenging than I had imagined.

I thought back to other times of transition in my life — moving away from home to go to college, starting my first job, getting married, having a baby, watching that baby go off to college himself and burying family members. Each of these times of change caused a confusing plethora of highs and lows within me.

Since my earliest years, I have heard the ancient Bible stories. I grew up in church learning about David, Ruth, Jonah, Peter, and Paul. As a child in Sunday School, these men and women seemed little more than fairy tale characters, no different than Snow White or Robin Hood.

With transition on my mind, I began seeing my own struggles in the stories of many of these biblical characters. Instead of living flawless lives, they often made poor decisions, felt sorry for themselves, and lost their way. They struggled through times of grief, unbelief, and disappointment, yet triumphed because they kept their eyes focused on God.

The men and women in this devotional book have spoken to me through their courage, honesty, and determination to follow through on what they felt God was calling them to do. They have helped me navigate the paths of my transition times to find the new life God has for me on the other side.

My prayer is that you will find your story among theirs and that God will continue to work through each of us so that we can have the full life Jesus wants for us.

"I have come that they may have life and have it to the full."

(John 10:10, NIV)

Millicent Flake, M.Div.
Sugar Valley, Georgia
www.maflake.com

Chapter 1

Moving Through Disruption:

Mary, the mother of Jesus

Luke 1:26-56

"Mary was greatly troubled at his words and wondered what kind of greeting this might be."

(Luke 1:29, NIV)

I remember the moment the nurse told me I was pregnant with our son. After months of trying, it seemed impossible to believe that I would be a mother. But as the initial elation calmed down, another emotion arrived — panic. I knew next to nothing about babies. Everything in my life changed the moment the pregnancy test came back positive —and I was scared.

Nothing disrupts a family's life more than learning a new baby is coming. Even though my husband and I were over-the-moon happy with the prospect of parenthood, we were anxious about bringing home a tiny bundle who does little more than eat, cry, poop, and sleep. We did not have family close by and I worried that I would not know how to look after a newborn. We had to make changes to our home, work schedules and daily life.

Fortunately, when I found out I was pregnant, Keith and I were ready for a child— we had been married for two years and were financially and emotionally ready to become parents. But not everyone who finds out a baby is coming is elated over the responsibilities and lifestyle alteration that parenthood brings.

Having a baby was one of the biggest changes in my life, but other times of transition have brought about a wide range of emotions also. Starting a new job, watching my son go off to college, going through the deaths of my parents, and retiring from my job have all upended my life in varying ways.

Jesus' mother Mary was one of those women who was initially *not* overjoyed at finding out she was 'with child.' Instead of reading a pregnancy test, she was given the news from an angel, who told her she was "favored" for being unwed and pregnant. That would be shocking enough, but Mary was a good Jewish girl who had not been intimate with her fiancé Joseph, or any other man. She knew she was a virgin.

This news was not just an embarrassing mishap — Mary could have been stoned to death for her "indiscretion." And at first Joseph was not sure he believed her story about the angel.

Mary was greatly troubled at his words and wondered what kind of greeting this might be. But the angel said to her, "Do not be afraid, Mary; you have found favor with God. You will conceive and give birth to a son, and you are to call him Jesus. He will be great and will be called the Son of the Most High. The Lord God will give him the throne of his father David, and he will reign over Jacob's descendants forever; his kingdom will never end."

(Luke 1: 29-33, NIV)

I can only imagine the vast range of emotions Mary must have felt, from fear for her life, to joy over being chosen, to anger at Joseph for not trusting her. While we will never find ourselves in the same situation as Mary, most of us have been faced with an unexpected circumstance that disrupts our lives, altering everything in an instant. We might discover infidelity in a relationship, lose a job, have a serious accident, or get bad news from the doctor. Even happy life changes like marriage, a promotion, or moving can cause us to feel disoriented.

Mary was chosen by God for her special role as the mother of the coming Messiah, even though she would be considered young by today's standards. Looking at her story in Luke 1 gives us some insights on how to handle the disruptive changes in our own lives.

1. Mary admitted her conflicted emotions.

The first thing we see is that Mary was open with her feelings when the angel Gabriel told her she was going to have a baby. Luke tells us she was "greatly troubled" (Luke 1:29, NIV). More modern translations say that she was *'confused,'* or *'perplexed,'* but I like *'troubled.'* She was probably *freaked out!* She knew enough about the birds and the bees to question the angel about how this could happen to her. She could not wrap her brain around the angel's words.

We need time to adjust to life changes, and sometimes we feel uncomfortable admitting our fears and anxieties. I remember talking to a woman who had twin girls who were grown. She said that for the first year of their lives, she was so overwhelmed she cried every day. Being honest with our emotions allows us to be able to get help if necessary.

Thirty-three years later, Mary's son Jesus would promise us:

"Peace I leave with you; my peace I give you. I do not give to you as the world gives. Do not let your hearts be troubled and do not be afraid." (John 14:27, NIV)

When we admit to God and others our fears, we allow God's peace to come in and comfort us.

2. Mary trusted that God would be with her.

Even though she was confused and frightened, Mary took the leap of faith that God would take care of her. When she asks Gabriel how she can be with child when she is a virgin, he replies:

"The Holy Spirit will come on you, and the power of the Most High will overshadow you. So the holy one to be born will be called the Son of God. Even Elizabeth your relative is going to have a child in her

old age, and she who was said to be unable to conceive

is in her sixth month. For no word from God will ever

fail." (Luke 1:37, NIV)

The angel encourages her not to be afraid, for *"Nothing is impossible for God."* (Luke 1:37)

I can imagine that Mary had no concept of what Gabriel's words meant. How could a teenage girl take all this in? Yet she accepts the angel's words and says,

---

"I am the Lord's servant. Let it be with me just as you

have said." (Luke 1:38)

Changes in life carry many unknowns, and that is what makes them so daunting. We know what our life is like before the baby or the empty nest or the loss of our loved one, but the new road ahead is not clear. In Psalm 139:5, God promises to go before us and to come behind us. Knowing that he will be with me no matter what the future holds gives me peace to move forward.

3. Mary shared her fears with someone who would understand.

Finally, in her bewilderment and worry, Mary turns to an older woman who can offer her a shoulder to lean on. After hearing this life-changing news from Gabriel, she quickly goes to visit her relative, Elizabeth. Elizabeth was past childbearing age but had also found herself unexpectedly pregnant. Of all the people, she was the only one who could remotely understand what Mary was feeling.

Mary got up and hurried to a city in the Judean highlands. She entered Zechariah's home and greeted Elizabeth. When Elizabeth heard Mary's greeting, the child leaped in her womb, and Elizabeth was filled with the Holy Spirit. With a loud voice she blurted out,

"God has blessed you above all women, and he has blessed the child you carry. Why do I have this honor, that the mother of my Lord should come to me? As soon as I heard your greeting, the baby in my

womb jumped for joy. Happy is she who believed that

the Lord would fulfill the promises he made to her. "

(Luke 1:39-45, NIV)

Elizabeth's baby, who would become John the Baptist, "leaps" in her womb at the sound of Mary's voice and Elizabeth is filled with the Holy Spirit. Elizabeth affirms what the angel said about Mary's coming child. She builds Mary up by letting her know how blessed she is for believing what God has said (Luke 1:45). After weeks of fear and turmoil, Elizabeth's words of encouragement must have felt like a balm on Mary's battered soul.

My older sister was the one I looked up to as a role model during my growing up years. She passed away from cancer when I was seventeen, and I was lost without her there for guidance. But through the years God has put mature, godly women in my life to help me through life's ups and downs. I am thankful for them. They have the insight that comes from years of trusting God and have shown me how to navigate uncertain waters.

In the same way, Elizabeth gives Mary the confidence she needs to embrace the assignment God has given her. In her beautiful *Song of Mary* found in Luke 1:46-55, Mary can finally say:

"With all my heart I glorify the Lord!"

(Luke 1:46, CEB)

Thanking God for even the smallest things can help us climb out of depression when life pulls the rug out from under us. Through prayer, God can help us see the good in even the most difficult situations.

Mary teaches us how to face new and uncertain times in our lives. We need to be open with our feelings, trust that God will take care of us even if we don't see the way ahead and talk to trusted friends who have been through similar circumstances. Then we, like Mary, can praise God no matter what comes our way.

Prayer: Abba Father, thank you for the time of life you have put me in right now. Help me to be patient with myself as I accept the emotional ups and downs that come with change. Remind me of your presence with me always and help me to feel your loving care. Amen.

Questions to ponder:

What feelings about my current situation am I ignoring? Have I been pushing down fear, anger, or uncertainty that I need to bring to God?

Ask yourself, who could I talk to who would understand what I'm going through and could give me godly counsel? Pray for God to open a door for a trusted friend to who has walked the same path you are now facing.

Chapter 2

Moving Beyond Disappointment:

David

I Chronicles 17

"Go and tell my servant David, This is God's word on the matter: You will not build me a 'house' to live in."
(I Chronicles 17:4, MSG)

I do not like to be told *no*. One of the hardest lessons I've had to learn in my thirty-five plus years of marriage is that I don't always get my way. It never seems to get easier.

I especially do not like to hear *no* from God. Several times in my life I thought I was going down the road God wanted for me when — bam! — I hit a roadblock and have to change direction. I'm left feeling angry and confused, wondering *why*.

> *When was the last time you heard God say no?*
>
> *How did you respond?*

When I'm frustrated over these changes in direction, I often think of one of my role models, Maurine Britenburg. Mrs. Britenburg was one of the strongest Christians I have ever known, yet she heard *no* from God, and struggled with it all her life.

I first met Mrs. Britenburg in 1982 when I was a young seminary student working as the youth minister at Highland Hills Baptist Church in Fort Thomas, Kentucky. Her husband had recently died and the wise minister of the church, Dr. Kruschwitz, arranged for me to stay with her on the weekends when I drove up from Louisville. He knew that she needed some company, but I received much more from getting to know her and seeing how she lived out her faith.

Mrs. Britenburg felt God's call on her life from the time she was a girl growing up in western Kentucky in the 1920s. As a teen, she fell in love with a young man who was equally committed to serving God, and they made plans to marry and become missionaries. She envisioned a life ministering beside her husband and sharing their love of Christ wherever God chose to send them.

But her life did not go as planned. As she told me the story fifty years later, tears still came to her eyes. For some reason, her father was against the match and forced her to break off the engagement. She was heartbroken.

The young man married someone else, and Mrs. Britenburg's family moved to northern Kentucky. After her father's death, she helped support her mother and sister through her work as a schoolteacher, moonlighting at a shoe store in the evenings. When World War II took many of the men away, she became a school principal, and was a no-nonsense leader.

In her late thirties, she was courted by the widowed Dr. Britenburg, a respected local physician. He convinced her to marry him and be a mother to his teenage son. This was the 1950s, and married women seldom worked, so she quit her job and became a full-time homemaker. Having lived all her life on a teacher's salary, she was suddenly the wife of one of the wealthiest men in town. They had a son of their own and lived a happy life until his death from cancer soon before I met her.

Mrs. Britenburg never lost her passion for serving God and through the years she taught children in Sunday School, led Vacation Bible School, and held many other jobs in her church. As she became older, she gave up working with the children due to her failing eyesight. But she felt called to be a prayer warrior and prayed every day for the church, its staff, and members. She touched countless lives, including mine at a time when I needed guidance.

Despite her love for her husband, son, and stepson, and the comfortable life Dr. Britenburg gave her, she still grieved the ministry she had envisioned for herself as a pastor's wife. Why did God say *no?* She would have been wonderful in that role, and her heart was in the right place.

Now that Mrs. Britenburg has gone to heaven, I know her questions have been answered! But on this side of heaven, we still struggle with having our plans thwarted.

King David in the Old Testament was one of God's special people, but he was told *no* by God. Reading in I Chronicles 17, we see David arriving at the pinnacle of his success as the new king of Israel. He has accomplished one of his goals by bringing the Ark of the Covenant back to Jerusalem.

The Ark was a gold covered chest containing the original tablets on which the Ten Commandments were written. It symbolized God's presence with his people, but the Philistines had stolen it from the Hebrews years before. Not having the Ark with them felt like God had left their presence.

Even after the Israelites retrieved it, this most holy artifact sat neglected for years in a private shrine in an out-of-the-way place. In one of the most moving scenes in the Old Testament, David dances joyfully and "with all his strength" as the procession returns with the Ark to Jerusalem (2 Samuel 6:14). All the people (except his wife Michal), cheer and rejoice as they march through the streets and deposit the Ark in a special tent.

David was now at peace with his enemies and settled into his new home. But he was always looking for his next project. He looked around at his elaborate and comfortable palace and realized that God's Ark was in a tent. *This isn't right!* he thought. *I need to build a beautiful house for God!*

He shared his idea with his trusted advisor Nathan, who tells David he should go for it. But that night God came to Nathan and told him to tell David this:

But that night, the word of God came to Nathan, saying, "Go and tell my servant David, This is God's word on the matter: You will not build me a 'house' to live in. Why, I haven't lived in a 'house' from the time I brought up the children of Israel from Egypt till now; I've gone from one tent and makeshift shelter to another. In all my travels with all Israel, did I ever say to any of the leaders I commanded to shepherd Israel, 'Why haven't you built me a house of cedar?'

(I Chronicles 17:3-6, MSG))

I can only imagine how crushed David felt when God said no. And to add insult to injury, God questioned why David would even *think* of building a house of cedar for him.

God tells David that while he appreciated all that he wants to do for him, he does not need a "cedar temple." With so much unrest in the land, the timing was not right for such an undertaking. The building of a physical temple will be the job of David's son Solomon, God says, who will be a man of peace, not a man of bloodshed like David.

When someone refuses our good intentions, it can feel like they are rejecting *us*. Perhaps David felt rejected by God. But in the next verses, God reassures him of his continuing love:

This is what the Lord of heavenly forces says: "I myself took you from the pasture, from following the flock, to be leader over my people Israel. I've been with you wherever you've gone. I've eliminated all your enemies before you. Now I will make your name great—like the name of the greatest people on earth". (I Chronicles 17: 7-8, CEB)

God lets David know that he has something even greater in store for him — David's name will endure forever.

Even though God said *no* to David, he knew David's heart and loved him for having the desire to please him. Let's look at what we can learn from David about handling those times in our lives when God seems to block our path.

1. We need to remember that just because something is a good idea, it may not fit with our talents or our calling from God.

David had a heart for pleasing God and on the surface, building a grand temple for God seemed like a good idea. But the timing was not right, and David was not the best person to do it. His son Solomon, who would eventually build the famous temple, was more suited to this type of project.

I had a seminary friend who was a quiet, studious young man who wanted to become a preacher. The problem was that he did not like public speaking. He decided to become a lawyer and I am sure he has been used by God in his career. Even though becoming a preacher was a wonderful goal, it may not have been best for him.

We are all bombarded with opportunities to do good things for God. Sometimes we can feel guilty if we do not volunteer for every job at church or give to every cause that comes along. Yet for each of us, our time and resources are finite, and we need to use them wisely.

A demonstration of the Spirit is given to each person for the common good. A word of wisdom is given by the Spirit to one person, a word of knowledge to another according to the same Spirit... All these things are produced by the one and same Spirit who gives what he wants to each person.

(I Corinthians 12:7-8, 11, CEB)

God does not call us all to the same ministry but uses all our gifts to build his kingdom.

2. When facing decisions regarding what direction we feel God is leading, we need to come before him with a submissive prayer for his guidance.

Despite David's disappointment in God's *no*, he accepted Nathan's words with grace and humility. Instead of lashing out in anger or vowing to forge ahead anyway, he is thankful for all God has done for him and prays:

"Who am I, Lord God, and of what

significance is my family that you have brought

me this far?"

(I Chronicles 17:16, CEB)

David made many wrong turns, yet he always loved God and was repentant for his actions. God knew David's heart, and God knows ours. When facing decisions, we must continually pray for God to take our egos and desires out of the equation so that we can discern his perfect will. This does not happen overnight, and like David, we will make mistakes along the way. But if our hearts are in a place of submission, we will hear God's leading.

22

3. Finally, we need to recognize that God may have something far greater in store for us than the plans we have for ourselves.

David's son Solomon eventually built the great temple that David had envisioned. For hundreds of years, it stood as the center of Israel's life until it was destroyed by the Babylonian king Nebuchadnezzar in 586 BC. Today only remnants of it remain.

God had something in store for David's legacy that would reach beyond a temple:

When the time comes for you to die, I will

raise up a descendant of yours after you, one of your

own sons, to succeed you, and I will establish his

kingship. He is the one who will build me a temple,

and I will establish his throne forever.

(I Chronicles 17:11-12, CEB)

David's lineage would produce Jesus, the Messiah who would save the world and who lives in our hearts today. How much greater is that than a monument of stones and mortar!

God's gentle *no* to David to build a temple for him speaks to me on a personal level. It reminds me that God's *no* does not mean that he doesn't love me, but that he has a greater vision than what I can imagine.

"Now to him who is able to do immeasurably more than all we ask or imagine, according to his power that is at work within us, to him be glory in the church and in Christ Jesus throughout all generations, for ever and ever! Amen."
(Ephesians 3:20-21, NIV)

I have clung to this verse many times in my life when faced with roadblocks in my path and it inspires me to keep going.

If Mrs. Britenburg had married the young preacher, she would not have moved to Fort Thomas, where she touched the lives of so many children and adults, including myself. Even if we do not always understand, God has a plan, and that comforts me when doors close.

Prayer: Dear Lord, thank you for always loving me and for sometimes telling me 'no'. Help me to come before you in humility and to ask for your guidance before making decisions. Give me patience and understanding with your ways. Amen.

Questions to ponder:

What decision you are facing right now that you need to bring before the Lord? Are you allowing pride and a need for accolades get in the way of what God may have for you to do? Think about how the outcome of the decision will best use your gifts and time.

Are you harboring anger over past decisions that may not have gone the way you wished? Bring your feelings before the Lord and ask for forgiveness and clarity.

Chapter 3

Moving Beyond Despair:

Mary Magdalene

John 20:11-18

"Among them were Mary Magdalene (from whom
seven demons had been thrown out) ... and many others who
provided for them out of their resources".
(Luke 8:2b-3, CEB)

Call me strange, but I enjoy reading obituaries of people I have never known. I think of it as honoring the person's life.

I especially love the ones that give little snippets of how the person lived. I might learn that he or she liked to fish or had a special pet. One obituary mentioned how much everyone would miss Mama's lemon pound cake.

I recall reading about a man who was remembered for his work as a parking lot attendant at his church. I picture this elderly gentleman watching for visitors on Sunday mornings, helping little ones out of their cars, and providing a welcome to all. Perhaps he stayed behind and missed the service to make sure everyone's car stayed safe. In life's grand scheme, his job seems small, but he found his identity in this servant role.

Having a servant's heart is difficult. No matter how much I strive and pray for it, I sometimes feel resentful when I am overlooked or unappreciated.

Maybe you feel this way at times. You might have a boss who takes credit for your work, or you are at home looking after small children who make mess after mess. We can often feel like no one knows the effort we put forth in our work, home, and church life.

When was the last time you felt unappreciated or overlooked for something? What emotions did this bring out in you?

Mary Magdalene was one of Jesus' followers who may have felt unappreciated for the efforts she put forth. We first read about her at the beginning of Luke 8.

Soon afterward, Jesus traveled through the cities and villages, preaching and proclaiming the good news of God's kingdom. The Twelve were with him, along with some women who had been healed of evil spirits and sicknesses. Among them were Mary Magdalene (from whom seven demons had been thrown out), Joanna (the wife of Herod's servant Chuza), Susanna, and many others who provided for them out of their resources. (Luke 8:1-3, CEB)

A few things stand out for me with this group of women. They had all struggled and been cured *of evil spirits and diseases*. And they were using their own money and resources to support Jesus and his ragtag group of disciples. Mark tells us more specifically that these women "cared for Jesus' needs" (Mark 15:41). They were not just "groupies" following Jesus for what he could do for them— they were an integral part of the team.

Luke mentions three by name: Mary Magdalene, Joana, and Susanna. Mark adds Salome and Mary, the mother of James and Joses. We also know Jesus' mother, Mary, was among the group.

Mary Magdalene is named each time the group of women come up, so she must have been special. All we know about her from the Scriptures is that she had seven demons purged from her (Luke 8:2). We don't know what these demons were, but they could have caused her physical symptoms similar to epilepsy. She may have suffered from schizophrenia or some other mental disorder.

Mary Magdalene is often confused with the prostitute who brought expensive oil and used it to wipe Jesus' feet in Luke 7 or portrayed in fictional accounts such as *Jesus Christ Superstar* as a fallen woman in love with Jesus. She may or may not have been a prostitute, but we can assume that the havoc the evil spirits in her life created would have caused her to be ostracized from the community. People would have kept their distance, both physically and emotionally. She may have been forced to live outside the city walls in utter poverty. Her family would have cut her off.

Imagine how hopeless Mary felt when she looked at her future.

Then Jesus came along and saw the true person inside Mary's demon-possessed body.

With compassion, Jesus freed her from her prison and restored her to life. Through the motley band following Jesus, she found a group of friends who respected and cared for her. Is it any wonder she devoted herself to caring for him and his disciples?

> *Who are some people in your life who have looked past your problems and accepted you for who you truly are?*

Mary Magdalene and the other women gave of themselves and their own money to make sure Jesus and the men had food, a warm fire at night, and a place to sleep. They toted water from a creek or well, found someone willing to sell them bread, and washed clothes in the river.

Perhaps they knelt before Jesus and the disciples to wash their feet at night after a long dusty walk. They may not have gone to sleep until after they knew the men were settled.

As she lay exhausted on her pallet at night, did Mary ever resent being a servant to the disciples? Did she wonder if her part in supporting Jesus and his work was worth it or noticed by anyone?

We know from what happened after Jesus was crucified that he noticed.

Mary Magdalene and the other women were there when Jesus and the disciples met in the Upper Room to celebrate their last Passover together. They would have served the meal and stayed to clean up as the men left with Jesus to go pray in the Garden of Gethsemane.

Then they heard the horrible news —Jesus had been arrested!

The men scattered, but the women watched from a distance as the unthinkable unfurled before their eyes. John tells us that Mary Magdalene and the other women stood weeping under the cross as their beloved Jesus was nailed to the cross and gave up his last breath. (John 19:25) In shock and grief, they may have gone with Joseph of Arimathea and Nicodemus as they took Jesus' battered body and placed it in the burial cave.

We can only imagine what was going through the minds of Jesus' faithful followers on that dark night. *Where would they go next? Were the soldiers coming for them? How could they survive without Jesus?*

The next morning, the men continued to cower in hiding, but the women went to the cave to tend to Jesus' dead body. Mary was the first one there and was shocked at what she found:

Early in the morning of the first day of the week, while it was still dark, Mary Magdalene came to the tomb and saw that the stone had been taken away from the tomb. [2] *She ran to Simon Peter and the other disciple, the one whom Jesus loved, and said, "They have taken the Lord from the tomb, and we don't know where they've put him."* (John 20:1-2, CEB)

Peter and John come running and confirm that what Mary said is true. The men go back to tell the others what they have seen, but Mary stays behind, sobbing and confused. *On top of everything else, has someone robbed even Jesus' body?*

She peers inside the tomb and sees two men wearing white, sitting where Jesus' body had been.

They asked her, "Woman, why are you crying?"

"They have taken my Lord away," she said, "and I don't know where they have put him." At this, she turned around and saw Jesus standing there, but she did not realize that it was Jesus. *(John 20:13-15, NIV)*

These verses bring a lump to my throat each time I read them. I see Mary completely wiped out, unable to take in one more bone-crushing attack. She has hit rock bottom with the events of the past days.

34

I wish I knew how Jesus looked in his new body that kept Mary from recognizing him. But she knew his voice.

Jesus said to her, "Mary."

She turned toward him and cried out in

Aramaic, "Rabboni!" (which means "Teacher").

(John 20:16, NIV)

In hearing Jesus say her name, everything changed for Mary. For the first time since they were all together in the Upper Room, she feels hope.

When has a word from God brought you up from a low and desperate place? You might hear his voice through prayer, from a loving friend, or by reading the Bible or other devotional material.

Mary is overwhelmed with joy, but Jesus tells her not to hold on to him, but to go tell the others that he has not yet gone up to heaven. She runs to the place where the other followers are holed up in fear and grief and announces the amazing news: *"I have seen the Lord!"* (John 20:18)

We don't know what happened to Mary Magdalene after that day, but we can assume that she was part of the group of women mentioned in Acts 1:14 who joined the men in constant prayer in the days before Pentecost. I imagine her continuing to serve others with even more zeal, sharing her stories of being with Jesus.

Mary Magdalene has always been one of my favorite biblical women. What can we learn from her life?

1. Mary Magdalene reminds me of all Jesus has done for me and to be thankful.

Jesus has saved me from my sinful nature and the many demons that lurk around me, just as he saved Mary Magdalene. Being by Jesus' side every day, I'm sure she never forgot the love, forgiveness, and acceptance she received from him.

I can get caught up in my daily problems and forget that I have that same love and forgiveness. Paul reminds us:

Rejoice always, pray continually, give thanks

in all circumstances; for this is God's will for you in

Christ Jesus.

(I Thessalonians 5:16-18, NIV)

Gratitude changes my outlook.

2. Mary Magdalene inspires me with her servant heart.

Mary shows me that no job is unimportant in the kingdom of God. She and the other women worked tirelessly behind the scenes so Jesus would have the strength and energy he needed for his mission. Being a parking lot attendant, keeping the nursery, or cleaning up after a church supper — all are necessary and valuable jobs in God's eyes.

Now you are the body of Christ, and each one

of you is a part of it. (I Corinthians 12:27, NIV)

God needs each of us doing our part for his work to get done. I need to remember this on those days when I feel that my work is menial or being taken for granted.

3. Mary Magdalene shows me that Jesus sees me and knows my heart.

Mary Magdalene went from being a servant at the bottom of the social strata to the person who was given the honor of being the first to meet Jesus in his resurrected body and to tell the others about it. At this time in history, women were viewed as little more than livestock, put on the earth to look after the men and children. But Jesus went outside the customs of the day and recognized the worth of each person, including a woman who was shunned by society. Mary's devoted heart was what mattered most to him.

God gave this faithful woman the reward he had been preparing for her by appearing to her first on that Easter morning. I am reminded that Jesus knows me by name and calls to me, just as he did with Mary. On those days when I feel discouraged, or in despair, I can go to him in prayer and know that I will be seen and heard. That gives me comfort.

Prayer: God, forgive me for the times I am resentful of others who seem to be getting the attention I crave. Help me to be thankful for all you have done for me and to be content with the peace that comes from knowing I'm working in your will. Amen.

Questions to ponder:

How can I be more like the women who followed Jesus and willingly give of myself, no matter how humble the task? Is there something I can do today to honor God and let others know through my life that Jesus is risen from the grave?

Paul tells us, *"Let's not get tired of doing good, because in time we'll have a harvest if we don't give up" (Galatians 6:9).* Pray for God to show you the blessings that are a result of the work you are doing, even if you are not aware of how you are touching others' lives.

Chapter 4

Moving Past Doubt:

Joseph, the Father of Jesus

Matthew 1:18-24

"Because he didn't want to humiliate her, he decided to call

off their engagement quietly."

(Matthew 1:19, CEB)

My aunt Grace used to say that she had a two-year pregnancy with

her first daughter Garner. She wasn't physically pregnant for that long —

how terrible — but she and her husband Russell were on the waiting list

for two years at the Children's Home Society of North Carolina to adopt

a child. They were thrilled when Garner came into their life as an infant.

Three years later they adopted another baby girl, LeeAnne.

For most of my life Garner and LeeAnne were the only adopted children I knew. It was never a secret in our family, and Grace and Russ doted on their daughters. Although in later years both Garner and LeeAnne were able to meet their biological families, they always knew that Grace and Russ were their parents. Grace and Russ had chosen them, and they knew they were loved.

We sometimes forget that Jesus was an adopted child. Joseph was not his biological father, yet, like my uncle Russell, he chose to be a good father to Jesus. But while Russell was thrilled to become a father, Joseph had to struggle through doubt to reach the place where he could support Mary.

Although little is written about Joseph in the New Testament, we learn much about him from just sixteen verses in Matthew. We know from his genealogy in the first chapter that he came from a long and noble Jewish family, going all the way back to King David. But Joseph's spirituality must have been deeper than just following what his family believed. His faith would be tested in ways he never imagined.

As their story begins in Matthew 1, Mary and Joseph are engaged to be married.

This is how the birth of Jesus Christ took

place. When Mary his mother was engaged to Joseph,

before they were married, she became pregnant by the

Holy Spirit. Joseph her husband was a righteous man.

Because he didn't want to humiliate her, he decided to

call off their engagement quietly.

(Matthew 1:18-19, CEB)

In biblical times, an engagement carried the same legal weight as today's marriage certificate. Money was exchanged between both families and a formal agreement was signed. Even though the wedding would not occur for another a year or two, the couple were not to consummate the marriage until after the wedding day.

We can only imagine Joseph's shock and devastation when his sweet fiancé Mary tells him that she is pregnant. Joseph has kept his vow of celibacy during the engagement, so he knows he is not the father of Mary's baby. He must assume she has been with another man.

They live in a small community, and his mind goes through the list of all the men who could have done this. *Maybe someone has raped her* he thinks with growing rage. He berates Mary to tell him truth: *When and how did this happen?*

The pain of infidelity hits deeply in the heart of anyone who has been on the receiving end. The sense of betrayal of this most intimate part of a man and woman's relationship is difficult to overcome. Joseph must have felt fury and the desire for revenge

Joseph knew the law: a betrothed woman who was found to be unfaithful could be stoned. He would have been entirely within his legal rights to bring Mary before the town and expose her betrayal. Their engagement would have been terminated and Mary would have been labeled as an adulterous woman. She and her family would have been humiliated and no man would ever want to marry her. Joseph would have been viewed as the injured party and been able to go on with his life, probably marrying another young girl in the village.

In these few verses in the first chapter of Matthew, I feel Joseph's agony as he sees no clear path ahead of him. He must have wondered how he could believe Mary's admonition that she had not been with another man.

Perhaps Joseph prayed like the father who brought his sick son to Jesus to be healed,

---

"I do believe; help me overcome my unbelief!"

(Mark 9:24 NIV)

I picture Joseph falling to his knees, begging God for guidance. He is torn between the teachings he has followed all his life and his love for Mary — between his head and his heart.

Have you ever doubted the word of a friend or loved one?

When have you been in a situation that caused you to fall

on your knees for clarity in taking the next step?

As we grow in our spiritual lives, we will inevitably be confronted with decisions that cause us to grapple with what we have been taught. Like Joseph, our head and our heart may be telling us different things.

What can we learn from Joseph about moving through times of doubt?

1. Keep moving forward.

We see from Joseph's example that at times of confusion and doubt we need to keep moving forward to the best of our ability. Joseph stood by his principles, even when his world was crumbling around him. He may have wished he could just ignore the situation, but that would have meant stoning for Mary. The best outcome he can see is to quietly end their engagement and hope for the best.

Sometimes when we are faced with a seemingly impossible situation, we have to plunge in with the best decision we can, trusting God to take care of us along the way. Times like these remind me of driving down a dark road at night — I can only see as far as my headlights, but I keep moving slowly forward.

2. Do not let fear take over.

As Joseph agonizes about how to handle the situation, he is visited in a dream by an angel. This messenger tells him to *not be afraid* to take Mary as his wife. Then the angel says something unbelievable — the child Mary is carrying is from the *Holy Spirit.* Wow.

But after he had considered this, an angel of the Lord appeared to him in a dream and said, "Joseph son of David, do not be afraid to take Mary home as your wife, because what is conceived in her is from the Holy Spirit. She will give birth to a son, and you are to give him the name Jesus, because he will save his people from their sins. All this took place to fulfill what the Lord had said through the prophet: "The virgin will conceive and give birth to a son, and they will call him Immanuel" (which means 'God with us').

(Matthew 1:20-2, NIV)

Throughout the story of Jesus' birth, the angels say, "*Do not be afraid.*" They give this command to Mary, to Zechariah in the temple, and to the shepherds. *Even though nothing makes sense right now, trust in God,* is their message. "*Choose* not to fear."

Do you think it is possible to choose courage over fear?

When have you had to 'buck up' and choose to be courageous?

Choosing not to be afraid may not be possible in our own strength, but with God's power, anything is possible. This verse from Paul is one I cling to when hanging on to the end of my rope:

"I can endure all these things through the power of

the one who gives me strength."

(Philippians 4:13, CEB)

The power to endure does not come from within me, but from the Holy Spirit when I give my problems over to him.

After the angel's visit, Joseph sees the way forward and makes the decision to take Mary as his wife and raise her son as his own. Joseph took good care of his new family. When he and Mary must make the trip to Bethlehem for the census, he finds a donkey for Mary to ride and makes sure she has a private, dry place to give birth. Later, when he is told in a dream to take his young son and wife to Egypt, he leaves his home to protect the baby from Herod the Great. He supports them for the time they are in exile and only returns when he is told in another dream that it is safe. We know that he taught Jesus to be a carpenter and raised him to follow the Jewish laws and customs.

Jesus had a closer walk with God than anyone who has ever lived, but the influence of his earthly father helped mold him into the man he became. As Jesus' earthly father, Joseph instilled in him a respect for his heritage, gave him the example of how to be a good and caring man, and provided the security of a stable home. Perhaps it was Joseph's example of taking care of others that prompted Jesus as he was dying on the cross to look at his mother and ask John to care for her. (John 19:26-27)

I have known many men and women, like my aunt Grace and uncle Russell, who have loved and cared for their nonbiological children with their whole hearts. What a wonderful gift and legacy they give the children in their lives!

3. Remember that you are dearly loved as part of God's family.

Just as Joseph adopted Jesus into his family, God adopts us and makes us part of his heavenly family. In the same way that Grace and Russ were thrilled to become parents, God is excited to have us in his family.

"Long before he laid down earth's foundations, he had us in mind, had settled on us as the focus of his love, to be made whole and holy by his

love. Long, long ago he decided to adopt us into his

family through Jesus Christ.

(What pleasure he took in planning this!)"

(Ephesians 1:5, The Message)

These verses tell us that God chooses each of us to be his own sons and daughters and to inherit all that he wants to give us. Because of this, we can never lose his love, no matter what choices we make in life. That knowledge gives me confidence that God will be with me when I am facing complex issues.

Prayer: Dear Abba Father, thank you for adopting us into Your family. Thank you for our earthly fathers and for what we learn from them. Help us to trust Your guidance when faced with doubts and difficult decisions. Amen.

Questions to ponder:

Are you struggling with doubt right now? Pray for God to give you clarity and wisdom as you choose what to believe.

Are you facing a situation where you need to choose courage over fear? Ask God for the strength to follow your convictions and to stand confidently in His love.

Take a few minutes to meditate on the fact that you were chosen by God to be part of His family. How does that make you feel?

Chapter 5

Moving Through Grief: Naomi and Ruth

Book of Ruth

"Only the woman was left, without her two children and

without her husband."

(Ruth 1:5, CEB)

I was blessed with a wonderful mother-in-law. Bobbie was a little dynamo of a woman who fiercely loved her family, believed in telling the truth, and courageously faced the heartbreaks in her life. From the moment Keith and I were married, I was her daughter, and I always knew she would be there for me.

Bobbie was widowed at the young age of fifty-two when her husband Lester died from a heart attack. They had enjoyed a strong and loving marriage, and she never quit missing him. Just a few months before she died, she commented to me that she never thought she would live twenty years without him.

Despite her grief, Bobbie made a point to not idolize their life together. She was open with me about their disagreements and the anger she continued to feel over some decisions he had made. Through our many conversations, I saw her accept and work through her emotions as she transitioned to a life without Lester by her side.

What has been your experience with grief? Have you had to struggle through the deep loss of someone close to you?

What has been the hardest part for you?

In the Old Testament book of Ruth, Naomi is a woman in the depths of despair over the deaths of her husband and two sons. Although the short book is named for her daughter-in-law, the story focuses on Naomi's journey from hopelessness to finding joy and meaning in life again.

Naomi and her husband, Elimelek, were from Bethlehem. When a famine came to their land, they moved to the country of Moab with their two young sons to find food and work. Elimelek died, leaving Naomi to raise her sons alone. The boys grew up and married Moabite women, Orpah and Ruth.

Ten years later, no children had been born to Orpah and Ruth. Then both of Naomi's sons died. Naomi's whole family was gone, and she had no heirs. In simple words, the scripture states her tragic situation:

"Only the woman was left, without her two children and without her husband."

(Ruth 1:5, CEB)

How heartbreaking is this verse — *"Only the woman was left."* Can you imagine how lost and alone Naomi must have felt?

In biblical times, a woman was totally dependent on a husband or male family member to support her. So, on top of the emotional devastation of having her husband and sons die, Naomi must deal with the reality that she is in a foreign land and destitute. Her situation is bleak.

Naomi gets word that God has ended the famine in her home in Judah, so she decides to return to her clan. Her daughters-in-law, Orpah and Ruth, prepare to go with her. But as they start down the road, Naomi turns to the young women and tells them to return to their families.

They must have had a close and loving relationship, because Orpah and Ruth tearfully implore Naomi to let them go on with her. But Naomi knows they are young enough to still lead happy lives and tells them to stay with their own families and find Moabite husbands. She, however, feels her life is over.

"This is more bitter for me than for you, since

the Lord's will has come out against me."

(Ruth 1:13, CEB)

During times of grief, have you ever felt like Naomi that

God is against you?

We can feel crushed and defeated and wonder if God is there.

What has that been like for you?

Eventually Orpah kisses Naomi goodbye and turns back to Moab. But Ruth stays with her mother-in-law. In a well-known passage often used at weddings, she pledges that Naomi's people will be her people and Naomi's God will be her God.

"Where you go, I will go and where you stay, I

will stay." (Ruth 1:16, NIV)

Naomi gives in to Ruth's pleadings and the two women, one old and one young, continue the long trip to Judah.

Think about how comforted Naomi must have felt to have Ruth with her on the long trip back to Judah. She had prepared herself to be alone in her grief, but now she has the companionship and support of her daughter-in-law. Having Ruth by her side would also keep her connected to the memories of the life she had with her sons and husband in Moab.

Too often I am like Naomi and think that I must make the journey on my own. I put on a stoic face and determine that I will soldier through by myself and not bother anyone with my problems. By doing so I miss out on the blessings God has waiting for me.

Think of a time when you let someone else minister to you.

How did that feel to receive help?

The women make it to Judah, where Naomi is welcomed home with open arms. But even though she is back with her family, she is still grieving her deep losses and feeling punished by God. She no longer feels like *Naomi,* meaning 'pleasant,' but *Mara* meaning 'bitter.'

As she walks the familiar streets, Naomi may be thinking back to the excitement she, Elimelech, and their sons felt when they left Bethlehem those many years ago. I imagine them starting down the road to Moab with Elimelech proudly leading the way and the little boys running alongside the cart. With her family to look after, Naomi's days would have been full and happy. Now she has returned feeling alone and desolate.

But God has not deserted Naomi. In an effort to support herself and Naomi, Ruth goes out to gather wheat in the fields and is noticed by the wealthy owner, Boaz. It turns out that he is a distant relative of Ruth's husband and therefore has the responsibility of looking after her. They marry and have a son, Obed. Naomi's friends rejoice with her on the new grandson and heir for her family.

Naomi's story of navigating the difficult road of grief is not much different from what many of us face as we learn to live without those closest to us.

What can Naomi and Ruth teach us about coming out on the other side of loss to a place where we can feel joy again?

1. Acknowledging our need for others makes the road less lonely.

When my father began to decline from Parkinson's disease, I felt helpless living seven hours away. Like Naomi as she was leaving Moab, my mother did not want to burden me with all she was going through, including the heartbreaking decision to put my father in a nursing home.

But she and I needed each other during that hard time. In his last weeks I was able to be there and to support her when he died. Those were precious days for me.

Too often we do not want to see our loved ones suffering, so we try to protect them by doing it all ourselves. But just as Naomi needed Ruth to make the journey back to Bethlehem with her, we need caring people around us to be the face of God during our painful transition times.

When we are at our lowest times, God often comes to us through other people. I cannot count the times I have gotten a text, card, or phone call from someone just when I needed it most. Allowing God and trusted friends and family to walk our path with us can be frightening, but the rewards are great.

2. When going through a time of grief, hold on to the hope that better days are ahead.

Despite the grief that my mother-in-law Bobbie felt during the years after the death of her husband Lester, she was a happy person. She found joy in her family and friends and especially in being with her grandson Adam. She taught me important life lessons about being a good wife and mother, handling heartache, and dealing with the inevitable changes in life. I did my best to make sure she had what she needed and that she was involved in our family life. I was with her on the day she died, and I hope she felt that I was *"better to her than seven sons."* (Ruth 4:15)

When Naomi returned to Bethlehem, she did not see how life would ever get better for her. But by the end of the book, she is rejoicing with her friends over her grandson and feels hopeful for the future.

Grief does not follow a straight path but has many ups and downs. Yet we can find hope in the Psalmist's words, knowing that on those long and sleepless nights, the sun will rise for a new day:

Weeping may stay all night,

but by morning, joy!

(Psalm 30:5, CEB)

---

3. Remember that God has not forgotten you during your darkest hours.

God had plans for Naomi's family, just as he does for ours. When Naomi directed Ruth to glean in Boaz's fields, hoping to do some matchmaking, she had no idea how significant this union would be. Ruth and Boaz's son Obed grew up to become the grandfather of King David.

Many generations later, Jesus the Messiah was born, a descendant from the line of David. Ruth, the Moabitess and Gentile, has the honor of being one of four women to appear in the genealogy of Jesus as accounted by Matthew.

God does not forget us during our mourning but gives us an extra measure of love and comfort. One of my favorite verses is Psalm 34:18:

"The Lord is close to the brokenhearted; he saves those whose spirits are crushed." (CEB)

When we feel most alone, we can rest in God's loving arms.

As the Book of Ruth ends, I picture Ruth and Naomi loving on baby Obed and delighting in each new skill he acquires. Naomi is at peace, knowing that Ruth is provided for and that some part of her family will live on through Obed. We can have that hope for the future as well.

Prayer: Dear God, thank you so much for putting special people in our lives at the times we need them. Give us the courage to share our imperfections, shortcomings, and fears with those who care about us. And thank you for the hope we have in you for brighter days, even when we are overwhelmed with grief. Amen.

Questions to ponder:

Have you found yourself keeping your feelings bottled up and not allowing close friends and family to share your struggles? Make a vow to reach out to someone and let them know your pain. You may find that the path is easier with someone to help.

If you are going through a dark time, think back on the ways God has been present for you. You may have felt his presence through a note from a friend, a Bible verse that popped up or a special song that brought you comfort. Write these down in your journal and look back at them the next time you feel yourself washing away in sadness.

Chapter 6

Moving Past Depression:

Jonah

Book of Jonah

"At this point, Lord, you may as well take my life from me,

because it would be better for me to die than to live."

(Jonah 4:3, CEB)

One of my favorite book characters is Eeyore, from the Winnie-the-Pooh series by A.A. Milne. Eeyore is the pessimistic donkey who plods through life with his head down, always expecting the worst to happen. He is the opposite of Winnie-the-Pooh and Piglet, who see the

67

sunny side of any situation (especially if honey is involved). Even in happy times, Eeyore is always waiting for the other shoe to drop and for his bad luck to return.

If you live or work with an Eeyore, you may get frustrated at their perpetual gloomy view. Their glasses are always half empty, and they have little faith in the proverbial light at the end of the tunnel. Trying to get an Eeyore to see the silver lining in problems can be challenging. But if we view the Eeyores in our lives with compassion, we may see that they suffer from depression, leaving them little energy for even the smallest tasks.

> *Is there someone in your life who has a gloomy disposition like Eeyore? How does he or she affect your mood?*

The prophet Jonah was an Eeyore thousands of years before Milne conceived of the Hundred Acre Wood. At every turn in Jonah's story, he whines, complains, and sees doom ahead.

Despite Jonah's often-debilitating mindset we will see that God uses him to save an entire city and Jesus portrays him as an example of a godly man. Pessimists of the world, rejoice!

Jonah's story begins with God giving him a missionary assignment. Nineveh was the capital of Assyria, a country known for its brutality toward the Israelites. Nahum describes it as a *"city of bloodshed—all deceit, full of plunder: prey cannot get away" (Nahum 3:1)* It does not sound like an enticing place to visit!

God tells Jonah that the sins of Nineveh have come to his attention, and he wants Jonah to get up and go there and *"cry out against it." (Jonah 1:2)*

Jonah is not pleased with the job he has been given. Like Eeyore, I imagine him whining, "But I don't *want* to go to Nineveh!" He decides he will trick Jehovah. Instead of starting on the five-hundred-mile trip to Nineveh, he boards a boat going in the *opposite* direction toward Tarshish.

He has not been on the boat long when a great storm comes up. The boat is in danger of capsizing, and the sailors panic and cry to their gods for help.

In typical Eeyore fashion, Jonah does not appear overly excited about the impending doom of the ship. In fact, he goes below and falls asleep, perhaps reasoning that he needs to be rested in case the end comes.

The captain comes to Jonah's bunk and rouses him, imploring him to call on his Hebrew God for help. Meanwhile the frantic sailors have cast lots and the blame has fallen squarely on Jonah for the storm.

The boat is pitching dangerously as Jonah groggily climbs up on deck. The sailors are sure they are about to die and cry out to him, *"Who are you and what have you done to cause this evil?"* Jonah is honest with them.

Jonah said to them, "I'm a Hebrew. I worship

the Lord, the God of heaven—who made the sea and

the dry land."

Then the men were terrified and said to him,

"What have you done?" (The men knew that Jonah

was fleeing from the Lord because he had told them.)

They said to him, "What will we do about you

so that the sea will become calm around us?"

(The sea was continuing to rage.)

(Jonah 1:9-11, CEB)

In a rare show of courage for Jonah, he accepts responsibility and urges the sailors to throw him into the churning ocean.

Despite their fear, the sailors want to spare Jonah's life and continue to try to row toward the shore. But when it becomes clear that they cannot make it, they ask for forgiveness and heave Jonah overboard. The storm suddenly stops.

I am sure Jonah thought this was his end, but the Lord has not abandoned him. God provides a "great fish," the proverbial whale, to swallow Jonah. For three days and nights he sits inside the fish, thinking about his life and his rebellion towards God. He hits 'rock bottom.'

In the belly of the whale, Jonah prays to God.

"I called out to the Lord in my distress, and he

answered me.

From the belly of the underworld I cried out for

help; you have heard my voice."

(Jonah 2:2, CEB)

Think of a time when you felt like you were sitting in the stinking belly of a whale. Did you find yourself bargaining with God?

Jonah realizes how fortunate he is that God has chosen to save him and promises to do better. God tells the fish to spit him out on the shore. For a second time God instructs Jonah to take his message to Nineveh. This time Jonah obeys.

Nineveh is a huge city, but Jonah boldly plows ahead. He preaches to the people that their city will be destroyed by Jehovah in forty days. Perhaps God was already working on their hearts, because the stubborn Ninevites believe Jonah's prediction. The entire population fasts and puts on sackcloth to show their remorse for their sins. The king himself dons a sackcloth and puts out a decree that no one, not even the animals, are to eat or drink, in hopes that the city will be spared by the Israelite God.

God in his great compassion decides not to bring ruin to the Ninevites. Jonah has saved thousands from death through his obedience to God's command. He should be happy, right?

But not Jonah the whiner. Instead, he is mad at God for sparing the city! He is so angry that he tells God:

"At this point, Lord, you may as well take my life from me, because it would be better for me to die than to live." (Jonah 4:2-3, CEB)

When Jonah goes off to sulk, God continues to be merciful and makes a large shrub to grow and shade him from the sun. Finally, Jonah is happy about something!

He spends the night nursing his anger under the shrub. But the next morning, God sends a worm to chew it up and it dies. Jonah's brief respite is over as the relentless sun beats down. He again tells God that he wants to die.

Eeyores can sometimes try our patience, and God seems to have run out of his. He tells Jonah:

"You 'pitied' the shrub, for which you didn't work and which you didn't raise; it grew in a night and perished in a night. Yet for my part, can't I pity Nineveh, that great city, in which there are more than one hundred twenty thousand people who can't tell their right hand from their left, and also many animals?" (Jonah 4:10-11, CEB)

If God spoke to me in this way, I would be shaking under that shrub! The book ends here, so we do not know Jonah's response. But he seems like a poor example for us to follow. He disobeyed God by running away from his assignment, almost caused the boat crew to die, grudgingly preached to the Ninevites, and then complained when God saved them. On top of it all, he was so angry about the shrub being taken away from him that he wanted to die.

But Jesus saw Jonah in a different light. Fast forward to the New Testament when the Pharisees confront Jesus:

Then some of the Pharisees and teachers of the

law said to him,

"Teacher, we want to see a sign from you."

"He answered, "A wicked and adulterous

generation asks for a sign! But none will be given it

except the sign of the prophet Jonah. For as Jonah

was three days and three nights in the belly of a huge

fish, so the Son of Man will be three days and three

nights in the heart of the earth."

(Matthew 12:38-40, NIV)

Jesus did not view Jonah as an irritating Eeyore or condemn him for feeling depressed but *compared Jonah to himself.* That is amazing to me. I have often felt that my times of depression were a sign of being "unchristian." But Jesus had compassion and respect for Jonah.

What was so special about Jonah that Jesus saw his work as a forerunner to what he would do as Messiah? What can we learn from a pessimist like Jonah?

1. Jonah was honest with God and with himself.

Most of us want to show our best selves to the world, especially among our 'Christian' friends, but Jonah was just himself. Instead of pretending that he was elated with the assignment to go to Ninevah, he sprinted as fast as he could to avoid it! No one ever had to question what Jonah was thinking. His lack of pretense is refreshing.

God knows our hearts, so we might as well be honest with him. He desires honesty in our inmost parts.

"And yes, you want truth in the most hidden

places;

you teach me wisdom in the most secret space."

(Psalm 51:6, CEB)

God wants us to push aside the masks we show to others and expose our hearts to him. Jonah had no problem being genuine with God.

2. Jonah never forgot who his God was, even if he ran in the opposite direction.

When the storm was raging and the sailors were interrogating him, remember what Jonah said?

"I am a Hebrew. I worship the Lord, the God

of heaven, who made the sea and the dry land."

(Jonah 1:9, CEB)

Jonah was not ashamed of his God. He knew that his God had the power to create the storm and the power to still it. He just wasn't too excited about going to the evil city of Tarshish.

When I am going through hard times, keeping the Bible close helps remind me of God's power. I belong to God, no matter what happens.

These words bring me comfort when I am sitting in the belly of the whale, feeling forgotten by God:

"Don't fear, for I have redeemed you;

I have called you by name; you are mine.

When you pass through the waters, I will be

with you; when through the rivers, they won't sweep

over you." (Isaiah 43:1-2, CEB)

God didn't leave Jonah inside that whale, and he will not leave me either. Even though he was not always pleased with Jonah, he never took away his love and grace. This reassures me that God will be there with me during my times of running and whining.

3. Jonah teaches me that I am never alone in my despair.

Have you ever been so overwhelmed and burdened that, like Jonah, you felt death would be preferable to continuing to live in your circumstances? The heaviness of depression can lead us to this place of ultimate despair. But God promises to meet us at the times when we have lost all hope, and we see this in his care for Jonah.

During those times when I may not be feeling God's presence, reminding my *head* that I am not alone gets me through when my *heart* may be having a hard time acknowledging it.

Paul encourages me to give all my concerns to God in prayer, and his words give me peace:

Do not be anxious about anything, but in every situation, by prayer and petition, with thanksgiving, present your requests to God. And the peace of God, which transcends all understanding, will guard your hearts and your minds in Christ Jesus.

(Philippians 4:6-7, NIV)

Eeyore was fortunate to have friends like Winnie-the-Pooh and Piglet to balance out his gloomy attitude. They stood by him, and loved and accepted him, no matter how down in the dumps he got. In the same way, God always stands with us. Friends who love us through our hard times display the love of God here on earth.

Prayer: Dear God, thank you for always loving me, no matter how much I grumble and complain. Help me to continue to listen for your Word for me and to be willing to do whatever you ask, knowing that you will give me what I need to complete the task. Amen.

Questions to ponder:

Do you find yourself acting like Jonah at times, complaining about your circumstances? Ask God to help you change your attitude and to see the situation through his eyes.

If you are struggling with depression, pray for God to open doors for you to find help. Start with confiding your feelings to a trusted friend or pastor. Sharing with others often makes our problems feel smaller. This is especially important if you have thought about suicide. God can bring you through even the most hopeless times.

Chapter 7

Moving Beyond Abuse:

Abigail

I Samuel 25

"She was an intelligent and attractive woman, but her husband was a hard man who did evil things."

(I Samuel 25:13)

In our early years of marriage, Keith and I had a German Shepherd named Steffie who was sweet, gentle, and playful. She slept on our bed and guarded our little boy Adam as if he was her own puppy.

We were involved in dog training at the time and decided to buy a male German Shepherd named Gunner. Gunner came from a line of guard dogs and was not a mean dog but had a harder personality than Steffie. As a male, he quickly dominated her. When they played together, he knocked her over, grabbed her treats, and let her know he was boss. Due to Steffie's docile nature, she let him push her around.

We soon began to see a change in Steffie's personality. Instead of the fun-loving and affectionate dog she had been, she became listless. She no longer ran after her ball or jumped up and down with joy when we came home from work. Like a woman in an abusive relationship, she became depressed and cowed down.

We knew something had to change. It wasn't fair to Steffie to submit her to being constantly pushed around by Gunner. We made the decision to find another home for Gunner and Steffie was soon back to her happy self.

You may have someone in your life that makes you feel beaten down. He or she may be an overly demanding boss, a critical parent, or a hard-to-please spouse. In what ways has being around this person changed how you feel about yourself?

Like Steffie, I have struggled at times to stand up for myself when faced with someone running over me. The stress of being on the receiving end of an abusive or domineering person can make me question my worth and lead to emotional and physical turmoil. I've always admired those with the inner strength to stand up to challenging people.

Abigail in the Old Testament is one of those women who stayed strong despite being married to a man who did not treat her well. The writer of 1 Samuel 25 describes Abigail and her husband Nabal this way:

She was an intelligent and beautiful woman,

but her husband was surly and mean in his dealings—

he was a Calebite. (I Samuel 25:3, NIV)

Nabal was a wealthy landowner and I picture him strutting around the house in his long robe, ordering servants to his bidding. Since divorce was not an option in her day, Abigail probably tried to stay out of his way. Whatever warm feelings that may have initially attracted Abigail to Nabal had long ago been wiped away by his offensive behavior.

One day Nabal's men are shearing three thousand sheep near Carmel. From far away in the desert the sounds of bleating sheep and the calls of men can be heard as they round up the animals.

King David and his army are camped nearby. They have been keeping an eye on the work of the shepherds as they brought the sheep to the shearers. David tells his soldiers not to bother Nabal's men and to make sure no one else interferes with their work.

David knows that a time of feasting will begin when the shearing is completed. As king, he is used to getting what he wants, and he feels that he and his soldiers should be rewarded for guarding the shepherds.

He sends ten young men to politely inform Nabal that he and his army expect to be invited to the post-shearing celebration. David points out that his army has looked after the shepherds, and no one stole from them. His message to Nabal instructs him to give his men *"whatever you have on hand."* (I Samuel 25:8)

I've watched enough gangster movies to know that David is pulling a 'Tony Soprano' here. His nicely worded message to Nabal carries a threat – *"Invite us or else!"* But Nabal doesn't realize he is dealing with the king and responds angrily to David's representatives:

" 'Who is David? Who is Jesse's son? There

are all sorts of slaves running away from their

masters these days' he snarls. 'Why should I take my

bread, my water, and the meat I've butchered for my

shearers and give it to people who came here from

who knows where?' "

(1 Samuel 25:8-10, NIV)

When the messengers report back to David, he is livid. *"Put on your swords!"* he calls to his men and soon four hundred soldiers prepare to attack Nabal and his shepherds. Tensions are running high.

In a panic, one of the servants runs to Abigail and tells her what is happening.

"David sent messengers from the wilderness to give our master his greetings, but he hurled insults at them. Yet these men were very good to us… Now think it over and see what you can do, because disaster is hanging over our master and his whole household. He is such a wicked man that no one can talk to him."

(I Samuel 25:14-17, NIV)

Abigail immediately sees the seriousness of the situation. Nabal's narcissism has put their whole household in peril. She doesn't bother to consult her foolish husband, but quickly loads up a huge amount of food to feed David's army, including five sheep ready to be roasted on the spit, two hundred loaves of bread and hundreds of raisin and fig cakes. She sends the servants ahead with the spread and follows on her own donkey.

She comes upon David and his men in a mountain ravine. What a picture this is! All alone on her donkey, Abigail confronts the army of four hundred angry, hungry men. Her only weapons are her charm and a banquet feast.

Despite her pounding heart, Abigail descends from her donkey. With nerves of steel, she bows down on her face before the king. As the woman of the house, she takes the blame for Nabal's offense. She assures David that she did not know about the messengers he sent. If she had, she would have welcomed them warmly, and this whole misunderstanding would not have happened.

"Put the blame on me, my master! But please let me, your servant, speak to you directly. Please listen to what your servant has to say. Please, my master, pay no attention to this despicable man Nabal.

He's exactly what his name says he is! His name

means fool, and he is foolish!

But I myself, your servant, didn't see the young

men that you, my master, sent.

(I Samuel 25:24-25, CEB)

She then uses her quick mind to appeal to David's pride by commending him for holding back his soldiers from attacking her family:

I pledge, my master, as surely as the Lord lives

and as you live, that the Lord has held you back from

bloodshed and taking vengeance into your own hands!

But now let your enemies and those who seek to harm

my master be exactly like Nabal!

Here is a gift, which your servant has brought

to my master. Please let it be given to the young men

who follow you, my master.

(I Samuel 25:26-27, CEB)

She goes on to praise David for not having the "staggering burden" of the blood of Nabal's household on his hands and assures him that the Lord will give him a "lasting dynasty" for fighting the Lord's battles. And in a final bit of strategy, she reminds David to remember her when the Lord has brought him success.

I admire Abigail's shrewdness in handling David's ego. She flips the cards and makes the situation about how wonderful David has been in refraining from attacking her family. And she reminds him that she has brought dinner!

David is impressed by her poise and beauty and accepts her apology, acknowledging that if she had not intervened, *"not one male belonging to Nabal would have been left alive by daybreak."* (v. 34) He calls off the men and gladly takes the food she has brought. Catastrophe averted!

When Abigail returns home, Nabal is partying with his friends, oblivious that his wife has just saved him from death and destruction. But God has the final word.

When Nabal sobers up the next day and Abigail tells him what happened, his heart fails him, and he falls down comatose. Ten days later he is dead. David, never one to pass up on a beautiful woman, wastes no time in asking the young widow to become his wife. Abigail agrees and rides off into the sunset with the king.

Abigail inspires me with her heroic story. In a time when women were considered mere property, she stands out as a model of a strong woman. She could have let herself become trampled by Nabal, but she keeps a healthy sense of self and does not allow fear of what he might do affect her actions. She must have struggled to live with Nabal, yet she never lowered herself to his level. Her strength and ability to keep her head in a time of crisis saved the lives of her whole household.

What can we learn from Abigail about dealing with and moving through times when we are dealing with abuse?

1. Abigail shows us how to handle a fool.

The book of Proverbs has a lot to say about fools —

- *they don't like to listen to others but prefer to give their own opinions (18:2)*
- *their foolish talk brings destruction (10:14)*
- *they enjoy doing wrong (10:23).*

Abigail does not let Nabal the fool demoralize her. She keeps a sturdy sense of who she is and separates herself from him as much as possible. When a crisis arises, she takes matters into her own hands and deals with it.

Accepting that we cannot change another person's behavior is the most important step in dealing with an abusive person. Once we realize that the only control we have is over our own actions, we can make decisions on how to best take care of ourselves to remain healthy emotionally, physically, and spiritually.

Each person should test their own work and be happy

with doing a good job and not compare themselves

with others. Each person will have to carry their own

load. (Galatians 6:4-5, CEB)

Being a 'doormat' for another person's abuse is not how God wants us to live. As Paul says in the scripture above, we are ultimately responsible for ourselves and carrying our own load, with the help of the Holy Spirit.

2. Abigail does not allow herself to fall to Nabal's level.

Abigail could have gone to Nabal and lambasted him for putting them in such a dangerous predicament when she hears the news from the servant. A shouting match may have occurred that would have accomplished nothing.

Proverbs warns against trying to argue with a fool:

When the wise make a legal charge against the

foolish,

the fools shout, they laugh—there is no calm.

(Proverbs 29:9, CEB)

We can waste valuable energy by trying to get a foolish person to listen to reason. I imagine that Abigail had given up trying to be rational with Nabal and had learned to circumvent his moods. Her discernment in going after David without consulting her husband was the wise choice.

Keeping ourselves from responding with anger toward a fool takes self-control and prayer but retaining our own sense of peace and calm is more important than winning an argument.

3. Abigail shows wisdom and humility in her response to David.

Abigail knew that sounding the alarm and gathering up Nabal's men to fight the army would have been futile. The shepherds would have been no match for David's trained soldiers and would have likely been slaughtered. Instead, she comes to David with respect and a desire to reconcile. She does not weep and wail but appeals to his sense of honor and speaks to him with the respect his role as king requires. David does not brush her aside but listens and takes her words to heart.

The difference between true humility which glorifies God and unhealthy subservience which causes us to be weak is sometimes hard to distinguish. We need to remember that our source of strength comes from the Lord.

Humble yourselves before the Lord,

and he will lift you up.

(James 4:10)

When Christ is within us, we have the strength to take on the challenging people in our lives and move beyond to living in true freedom.

Prayer: Dear God, thank you for promising to give me strength no matter what my circumstances. Give me discernment and wisdom to know the best way to handle the foolish people in my life. Help me to always face difficulties with a clear mind and with my head held high, knowing that I am Your child. Amen.

Questions to ponder:

Is there a Nabal in your life who shows characteristics of a fool? Pray about your relationship to him or her and ask God to give you the strength, wisdom, and discernment to handle the situation.

Have you found yourself treating others in a belittling or angry way? Bow down before the Lord and ask Him to forgive you and to give you the conviction you need to change your behavior and treat others with God's love.

Chapter 8

Moving Beyond Defeat:

Peter

John 21:1-19

"Then he cursed and swore, 'I don't know the man!'

At that very moment the rooster crowed."

(Matthew 26:74, CEB)

I sat across from my friend at lunch as she shared her worries about her twenty-five-year-old daughter.

"I've learned not to ask too many questions," she said as she pushed her salad around her plate. "I'm not even sure where she is living. All she seems interested in is partying." Her voice was strained. "She wasn't raised this way. I'm ready for her to grow up."

My heart broke for my friend's feelings of helplessness over the choices her daughter was making. As parents, we want our children to be safe and happy and to fulfill the dreams we have for them.

The journey to maturity for us all is full of ups and downs. We hit potholes in the road which cause us setbacks and detours. As we watch our children navigate the road towards adulthood we often struggle because we see where *we* want them to be before they are ready to be there. Sitting back and letting them make their own mistakes is difficult.

The same is true of our path to spiritual maturity. Just as we see the potential in our own children, God knows where he wants *us* to be in life as we struggle along. Fortunately, he never gives up on us and is there to pick us up when we fall.

> *Think of a time that you faced defeat. Did you feel that you had let down yourself, others and/or God? What were your feelings?*

Simon Peter was one of the most well-loved of Jesus' disciples and a great example of someone who had highs and lows in his spiritual journey.

When we first meet him in Matthew 4:18, he is fishing with his brother Andrew. If Jesus had not come along, he would have lived his life in obscurity, raising a passel of kids and teaching them to throw their nets into the sea for the catch of fish.

But Jesus did come along and called Peter and Andrew to follow him. The brothers dropped their nets and followed the young rabbi. They could never have imagined what lay ahead.

From the beginning, Jesus saw leadership potential in Peter. He knew that beneath Peter's rough edges was an intelligent and passionate man who could relate to the common person. Jesus knew Peter was who he needed to lead his church— the *petra*, or *Rock*, on which he would build his kingdom. (Matthew 16:18)

Yet just as we see our children make mistakes and learn from them, Peter had to grow into the man Jesus saw. He had to overcome fear and weakness that could have destroyed him if not for Jesus' faith in him.

On the night that Jesus was to be betrayed and arrested, he and the disciples ate their Passover meal, then left for the Mount of Olives. (Matthew 26:31-35) Jesus knew his time with his inner circle was coming to an end. He warned them that it had been prophesied that none of them would stand by him.

Peter is irate, and cocky enough to think that he is better than all the other disciples. But Jesus knows that Peter still has maturing to do.

Peter replied, "If everyone else stumbles because of

you, I'll never stumble."

Jesus said to him, "I assure you that, before the

rooster crows tonight, you will deny me three times."

Peter said, "Even if I must die alongside you, I won't

deny you." All the disciples said the same thing.

(Matthew 26:33-35, CEB)

The disciples follow Jesus to Gethsemane, where the men fall asleep while Jesus pleads with God to have his cup taken from him. Peter is jolted awake to see Judas next to Jesus, and a mob carrying swords.

Before he and the others know what has happened, Jesus is arrested and led away to stand before the high priest. Matthew tells us:

"Then all the disciples left Jesus and ran away."

(Matthew 26:56, CEB)

Peter follows the crowd at a distance and hangs around in the shadows, hoping to hear news of what is happening. His bravado fades away as the reality sinks in that Jesus may not escape this time. We can only imagine the fear, anguish and confusion roiling around inside him. Their cause appears to be lost and all the disciples are in danger of being arrested.

Peter tries to stay out of sight, but a servant girl recognizes him as one of Jesus' followers. "Aren't you one of them?" she asks. Before he can stop himself, he angrily declares that he does not even know Jesus. Two more times someone accuses him of having been with Jesus, even commenting that his accent shows that he is not from Jerusalem.

A short time later those standing there came and said

to Peter, "You must be one of them. The way you talk

gives you away" Then he cursed and swore, "I don't

know the man!" At that very moment the rooster

crowed. Peter remembered Jesus' words, "Before the

rooster crows you will deny me three times."

And Peter went out and cried uncontrollably.

(Matthew 26:73-75, CEB)

My heart goes out to Peter. I have had times in my life when I felt I could never get past a blunder that let myself and God down. Surely this is the lowest point of Peter's life, and he must have wondered how he could ever hold his head up again.

But Jesus had not given up on Peter.

In John 21, we read the beautiful account of Jesus letting Peter know he has forgiven him for that awful night in the courtyard.

The disciples had watched Jesus die on the cross, but three days later he appears to them in his risen body. Despite their joy and excitement, they are not sure what to do next. Peter turns to what is familiar — he and several of the other men get into their boats and go fishing.

After a long night of throwing out their nets, they have not caught anything. They see a man on the shore who tells them to try casting their nets on the other side of the boat. Suddenly the net is so full of fish that they can barely pull it up. In astonishment, they realize the man is Jesus.

Overjoyed, Peter jumps into the water and swims toward his teacher. When he gets there, he finds Jesus tending to a small fire on the beach. Jesus tells him to bring some of the fish they have caught and proceeds to cook it over the coals. As the disciples arrive and awkwardly sit down, Jesus serves them fish and bread, in the same way he served them at the Last Supper.

They finish their breakfast and Jesus turns to Peter. Knowing that Peter denied him three times, Jesus gives him three opportunities to profess his love for him:

When they finished eating, Jesus asked Simon Peter,

"Simon son of John, do you love me more than

these?"

Simon replied, "Yes, Lord, you know I love you."

Jesus said to him, "Feed my lambs."

Again Jesus asks Peter:

"Simon son of John, do you love me?"

Simon replied, "Yes, Lord, you know I love you."

Jesus said to him, "Take care of my sheep."

I imagine Peter sitting with bowed head before Jesus, confused about where this conversation is headed. When Jesus asks the same questions a third time Peter's emotions overflow:

He asked a third time,

"Simon son of John, do you love me?"

Peter was sad that Jesus asked him a third time,

"Do you love me?"

He replied, "Lord, you know everything;

you know I love you."

Jesus replied, "Feed my sheep."

(John 21:15-19, CEB)

Jesus lets Peter know through this brief conversation that he still has plans for him. Peter is going to be instrumental in spreading the gospel across the world — he will be *feeding the sheep.*

Peter changes after this time on the beach. He grows into the man he was meant to be, letting go of the guilt that has held him down and putting his mind and heart to the task ahead.

When we next encounter Peter in the beginning of the book of Acts, he is the leader of the group of believers. The passion that he possessed as a younger man now merges with a newfound confidence which forges him into the rock that Jesus envisioned.

Despite lacking a formal education, he preaches at the synagogue and heals people in the name of Jesus. He goes against the Jewish hierarchy to fulfill that mission of bringing the gospel to the Gentiles.

Two thousand years later, we are still inspired by the letters he wrote to the early church, giving this assurance to the new Christians:

May the God and Father of our Lord Jesus Christ be blessed! On account of his vast mercy, he has given us new birth. You have been born anew into a living hope through the resurrection of Jesus Christ from the dead. (I Peter 1:3, CEB)

I find Peter the most relatable of all the disciples with his penitent heart. What can we learn from his life about maturing and moving past our defeats?

1. God meets us where we are on our path to maturity.

When Peter was a young man traveling around Galilee with Jesus and the other disciples, he was where he needed to be, even if he didn't always do it perfectly. As a more mature and seasoned Christian, he fulfilled God's role for him as the courageous leader of the movement that would change the world forever. And in his last years, he continued to encourage the church through his letters, which inspire us today.

I remember when I was in my twenties and training to be a hospital chaplain. I was told continually by my supervisors that I was *getting there*. I got tired of those words because I wanted to *be there*. I realize now that my mentors were letting me know that I was doing well but still had much to learn. Some growth can only come from life experiences.

Peter knew that growth takes time and comes in stages:

So don't lose a minute in building on what you've

been given, complementing your basic faith with good

character, spiritual understanding, alert discipline,

passionate patience, reverent wonder, warm

friendliness, and generous love, each dimension fitting

into and developing the others. With these qualities

active and growing in your lives, no grass will grow

under your feet, no day will pass without its reward as

you mature in your experience of our Master Jesus.

(2nd Peter 1: 5-8, MSG)

2. God always forgives our actions and *inactions.*

The times in my life that I look back on with the most sadness are

those times when I failed to do something that God was leading me to do.

Missed opportunities cannot be gotten back.

How often did Peter wish he could go back and change his responses on that dark night in Herod's courtyard? Did he imagine himself standing up to the crowd and saying, *"Yes, I'm one of his followers, what do you want to do about it?"*

In the book of Acts, we see Peter following the Holy Spirit by taking a very unpopular stance to accept Gentiles into the fellowship. In the same way he followed Jesus whole-heartedly as a young fisherman, he goes all in with his new assignment:

Peter fairly exploded with his good news: "It's God's own truth, nothing could be plainer: God plays no favorites! It makes no difference who you are or where you're from—if you want God and are ready to do as he says, the door is open. The Message he sent to the children of Israel—that through Jesus Christ everything is being put together again—well, he's doing it everywhere, among everyone."

(Acts 10: 34-36, MSG)

Peter's courageous stand on welcoming Gentiles into the faith changed the course of history for Christianity by making Jesus' teachings available to more than just the Jews of Palestine. Most of us would not be Christ followers if not for him.

3. When we come humbly before God and allow him to work in our lives, we cannot imagine what he will accomplish.

Who could have pictured Peter, a rough, uneducated Galilean fisherman, standing before a crowd of perplexed people from many different nations on the day of Pentecost and quoting Scripture to them to prove that the Messiah had come? (Acts 2)

I am comforted to know that no matter how I may let Jesus down by my action or *inaction*, he never gives up on me. Just as we see the best in our own children, I am my very best self in Jesus' eyes. When I come to him in humility and let him have control in my life, I feel the doors open for the work he has planned for me.

In a letter Peter wrote in his old age to the believers who were scattered throughout the region, he reminds them and us of our important calling:

But you are the ones chosen by God, chosen for the high calling of priestly work, chosen to be a holy people, God's instruments to do his work and speak out for him, to tell others of the night-and-day difference he made for you—from nothing to something, from rejected to accepted.

(I Peter 2:9-10, MSG)

Peter knew the joy of feeling God's hand on his life — that God could bring him from '*nothing to something, from rejected to accepted.*' We are chosen in the same way.

And my friend's daughter? Three years later she graduated from college, met a nice young man, and is now married with a child on the way. Through her mother's encouragement and prayers, she matured through her difficult early adult years.

Prayer: Dear God, thank you for loving me even when I am struggling and making mistakes. Help me to be patient with myself and others as I strive to please you and to be the person you want me to be. Thank you for putting me right where you need me today. Amen.

Questions to ponder:

Are you harboring guilt over failing God by something you did or didn't do? Go to him in humility and ask for forgiveness, then be willing to accept that forgiveness and let go of the yoke of guilt. Ask God to show you which direction he wants you to go next!

Do you know someone who is struggling to mature in their faith? Commit to pray for them and be open to ways you can support them in their journey.

Chapter 9
Moving Forward by Letting Go:
Paul

Philippians 3:13-15

"Together, they charged at Stephen, threw him out of the city,

and began to stone him. The witnesses placed their coats in

the care of a young man named Saul."

(Acts 7:57b-58, CEB)

My eyes popped open in the darkness, and I groaned when I saw

the time: *2 a.m.* I had a fleeting memory of dreaming about arguing with

a coworker at my job. Even though I had been retired for months, lingering feelings of guilt and despair washed over me. I lay in the dark as my heart continued to race, my mind turning over past words that couldn't be taken back.

Does this sound familiar to you? Do you find yourself, like me, struggling with feelings of remorse in the wee hours of the morning when the demons love to cavort? I've lost sleep over a thoughtless comment spoken in anger, an unwritten thank you note, or a failure to follow through on a promise. The sense of inadequacy can stay with me throughout the dy.

While my litany of shortcomings is largely inconsequential, I know people who live with actions or decisions that have resulted in serious repercussions — a car wreck that left someone permanently disabled, a bad investment that wiped out a family member's savings, a loss of temper that cost a friend his job. Others have left behind pain and suffering for their loved ones due to times of addiction or immorality. The guilt can linger for a lifetime.

What regrets and mistakes wake you up in the middle of the night? Do you struggle to forgive yourself? What are some actions from others that you have a hard time forgiving?

Paul in the New Testament knew something about remorse. Known as Saul in his former life as a Pharisee, he was committed to squashing the new Christian cult that was threatening to turn Judaism upside down. His zeal caused death and suffering for many followers of Jesus.

One day Saul came upon a mob shouting at a Greek man named Stephen, one of the Jesus followers that he hated. Stephen had been arrested for trumped up charges that he had spoken "blasphemous words against Moses and against God." (Acts 6:11, NIV) In a forceful sermon,

Stephen tries to convince his accusers that they have turned their backs on their faith and have committed a great sin by crucifying Jesus.

These are fighting words to the Jewish council members who are listening. They murmur among themselves, *Who is this Greek to tell us, the leaders of the temple, that we are wrong?*

The council's anger turns violent, and they grab Stephen. Instead of fighting back against them, Stephen sees a vision of heaven opening and the 'Son of Man' standing next to God. This further infuriates the crowd, which turns murderous:

The council members shouted and covered their ears.

At once they all attacked Stephen and dragged him

out of the city. Then they started throwing

stones at him.

(Acts 7:57-58a, CEB)

I have heard this story of Stephen's stoning all my life and I always imagined the men throwing little pebbles. But this was a brutal gang attack against a defenseless man. The crowd was throwing huge boulders on Stephen, breaking his bones until the rocks finally crushed his skull or suffocated him.

As Stephen is dying, Luke shares a chilling detail — Saul is watching the mob's attack but is too dignified to pick up a stone and throw it himself. He simply stands by as the men pull off their outer robes and lay them at his feet. While Saul nods his approval, they proceed to execute Stephen in cold blood.

The witnesses placed their coats in the care of a

young man named Saul. As they battered him with

stones, Stephen prayed, "Lord Jesus, accept my life!"

Falling to his knees, he shouted, "Lord, don't hold

this sin against them!" Then he died.

(Acts 7:59-60, CEB)

Even as his bones are being broken and his lungs are crushed, Stephen does not condemn his attackers. How could someone stand by on the outskirts of this violence and not feel remorse? Yet Saul applauds the death of one more Christ follower.

Not long after, Saul and his entourage are on the road to Damascus to find more Christians to take back to prison in Jerusalem. A blinding light knocks him down and he hears a voice asking, *"Saul, Saul, why are you harassing me?" (Acts 9:4, CEB).*

The speaker identifies himself as Jesus, but only Saul can hear the voice. When he looks up, Saul is blind and helpless. His friends take him to Damascus, where he does not eat or drink for three days.

God sends the disciple Ananias to confirm to Saul that it *was* Jesus who spoke to him. Ananias explains that Jesus wants Saul to be able to see again and to be filled with the Holy Spirit.

Immediately Saul can see, both physically and spiritually. He realizes that his zeal was misplaced. Just as he had once given his whole heart to persecuting Jesus' followers, he now commits himself to spreading the good news that Jesus has come as the Messiah.

Can you identify a specific "Damascus Road" experience when the Holy Spirit grabbed you and turned your life around? Or has your spiritual growth been more gradual and subtle?

Before his conversion to following Jesus, Saul, now known as Paul, was a prominent Pharisee and a top tier teacher of the law. He had worked hard for his position and had earned every accolade for being the best Jew possible.

In his letter to the Philippians, he shows his status as Saul of Tarsus:

We don't brag about what we have done, although I could. Others may brag about themselves, but I have more reason to brag than anyone else. I was circumcised when I was eight days old, and I am from the nation of Israel and the tribe of Benjamin. I am a true Hebrew. As a Pharisee, I strictly obeyed the Law of Moses. And I was so eager I even made trouble for the church. I did everything the Law demands in order to please God.

(Philippians 3:3b-6, CEB)

The next sentence is the basis of Paul's new life:

But Christ has shown me that what I once thought was valuable is worthless. (Philippians 3:7, CEB)

All his work moving up the Pharisaic ladder now meant nothing. Yet despite his dramatic turn-around, I wonder if Paul ever missed that old life. Did he think about his former students with whom he had shared his love of the Scriptures? Did he yearn for the discussions with his colleagues or the respect he received from those at the synagogue? What about his family, with whom he presumably cut ties? Did he grieve for those relationships?

Did he ever wake up in a cold sweat in the middle of the night with Stephen's stoning replaying in his mind?

If Paul ever experienced these feelings, he never let his regrets, pain, or guilt keep him from carrying out what he believed God was calling him to do. He overcame his demons by using the power of his great mind combined with his complete trust in God. Compared with all that Christ had given him, the perks of his previous life meant nothing to him anymore. (Philippians 3:7-9)

In one of my favorite passages, Paul uses a running metaphor to show how a believer can get tripped up if he or she looks back instead of forward in a race:

"Brothers and sisters, I myself don't think I've reached it, but I do this one thing: I forget about the things behind me and reach out for the things ahead of me. The goal I pursue is the prize of God's upward call in Christ Jesus."

(Philippians 3:13-14, CEB)

As a runner, I know I can lose valuable time in a race by checking to see who is behind me. I must keep my eyes on the road in front of me, or I risk stumbling. Paul knew that if he spent too much time dwelling on his past, he would miss what God had planned.

When bad memories threaten to trip us up, what does Paul teach us about keeping ourselves moving forward and not backwards in our spiritual lives?

1. We need to develop mental toughness and discipline.

Letting go of the past and focusing on the future is a *decision* that we make. We may feel that we can't control the thoughts that run through our minds, but we *can* make the choice of what we focus on. Paul knew that it was easy to be pulled into a downward spiral, so he gave us practical advice:

"From now on, brothers and sisters, if anything is

excellent and if anything is admirable, focus your

thoughts on these things: all that is true, all that is

holy, all that is just, all that is pure, all that is lovely,

and all that is worthy of praise.

Practice these things."

(Philippians 4:8-9a, CEB)

Spending time in prayer and Bible study each day and listening to Christian music and podcasts helps me keep my mind on "things that are excellent." In addition, we need to surround ourselves as much as possible with spiritual friends who build us up, not tear us down.

2. We need to set our priorities.

Continuing his running analogy, Paul tells us that he keeps his eye on the goal, or prize, that he is working towards.

"The goal I pursue is the prize of God's upward call in Christ Jesus." (Philippians 3:14, CEB)

Just as a runner competes to win a trophy, we need to remind ourselves that our ultimate goal is a deeper walk with God. As we pursue this, we will glorify Christ in our lives.

Paul worked extremely hard for the life he had as a Pharisee, but once he knew Christ, his former goals and aspirations meant nothing to him. When we see a glimpse of what God has in store for us, we realize that we do not have time to waste focusing on the past.

3. We need to remember that we do not have to do this by ourselves.

We may feel that we need to let go of painful memories and misdeeds through sheer force of our minds, but God does not leave us alone to push ahead. Paul reminds us that God will help us move to the next level of spiritual maturity.

So all of us who are spiritually mature should think this way, and if anyone thinks differently, God will reveal it to him or her. Only let's live in a way that is consistent with whatever level we have reached.

(Philippians 3:15-16, CEB)

When old "tapes" of painful memories begin to play in my head, I remind myself that they do not come from God, but from the *Accuser*, the devil who wants to see me fall. God has forgiven me for any past sins and has even forgotten them (Isaiah 43:25)! He does not want to see me wallowing in guilt but living in peace.

Letting go of the past, whether happy or painful, can be extremely difficult. We may need time to grieve, but there comes a point where we need to turn our heads and see what is waiting down the road. We must be patient with ourselves as we train our minds, keep our eyes focused on Christ, and allow God's presence to comfort us.

Prayer: God, help me to remember that accusing thoughts are not from you. Remind me that if I continue to focus on the guilt I carry, I will miss out on the exciting life you have in store for me. Forgive me for my past failures and point me forward to the blessings you want to give me. Amen.

Questions to ponder:

What does God want you to forget and leave behind today? Are you harboring blame for something that Christ has already forgiven? Ask God to remove the burden, then take a deep breath and experience the weight of guilt leaving you!

What lies ahead that God wants to show you today? Pray for him to show you the open doors he has in place for the work he wants to do in your life.

Chapter 10
Standing Firm:
Shiprah and Puah
Exodus 1:15-21

"But the midwives had far too much respect for God

and didn't do what the king of Egypt ordered;

they let the boy babies live."

(Exodus 1:17, MSG)

One of my favorite books as a young teenager was *The Diary of Anne Frank.* Like Anne at thirteen, I was the second of two girls, had crushes on boys and liked to write in my diary. I was deeply touched by the drama Anne shared in her notebook as she and her Jewish family were forced into hiding in the attic of her father's business in 1942. They spent two years confined to the secret annex with another family as the Nazis roamed the streets below in Amsterdam.

The secret hiding place was finally discovered and all the occupants were sent to concentration camps. Anne's father was the only one to survive. When he returned to the attic annex after losing his entire family to the Nazi death camps, he must have wondered what good could have come from the years they spent in hiding.

Anne's little notebook detailing her feelings and daily life in the attic had been left behind and was discovered by Mr. Frank. Her story was immortalized through the publication of the book, a Broadway play, and movie. She gave a face to the millions of Jews who died in the Holocaust. Anne's story touched countless lives, including my own.

She and her family would not have survived for as long as they did without the brave friends and coworkers who risked their lives to hide and support them. Without the courage of the many who defied Hitler, Anne's voice would never have been heard.

I have often wondered what I would have done if I had lived in Germany in the 1930s. Would I have been as courageous as the helpers of the Franks, or would I have turned a blind eye as my neighbors were forced into trucks and taken away by the German soldiers?

I am amazed when I read about people who are willing to put their lives on the line for their beliefs. Most of the time, I do not want to be *inconvenienced* for someone else, much less risk death.

When have found yourself in a situation where you needed to take a stand for your beliefs? How did you respond?

I am sad to say that often my hesitancy in standing up for my beliefs comes from fear of what others will think of me. I find it easier to keep going about my daily life and ignore injustices and prejudices around me. But is that what God would have me do?

As we journey through our lives, we may come to a place where we need to stop and stand firm.

Throughout the Bible we see people who bravely stood up for their beliefs, despite the consequences. Two women mentioned briefly in the Old Testament had the courage to put their own lives on the line to save the lives of Hebrew babies. Before the term *civil disobedience* was invented, these women carried it out by simply *not* doing what the authorities ordered. Their fear of disobeying God was stronger than their fear of death.

These women were the midwives Shiprah and Puah, and we read their story in the first chapter of Exodus in the Old Testament.

The Egyptian king was worried because the Hebrew slaves kept having more and more babies. Fueled by suspicion and his own insecurity, he was afraid that if their numbers kept getting larger, they might decide to side with his enemies and revolt against him. Just as Hitler became obsessed with getting rid of the Jews in modern times, Pharaoh decided he needed to take action against the Hebrew slaves.

134

Pharoah first tried working the slaves to death, but they continued to "multiply and spread." So, he decided that his best bet was to kill off all the Hebrew boys immediately after they were born. He needed the Hebrew midwives to do his dirty work.

He called in Shiprah and Puah and gave them their orders:

"When you are helping the Hebrew women

give birth and you see the baby being born, if it's a

boy, kill him. But if it's a girl, you can let her live."

(Exodus 1:16, NIV)

Pharaoh's order put Shiprah and Puah in a no-win situation. They had dedicated their lives to helping women bring their babies into the world, yet if they disobeyed the king, they could lose their own lives.

I imagine them sitting with their heads together that night, praying fervently and discussing what to do. They decided to disobey Pharaoh.

"The midwives, however, feared God and did

not do what the king of Egypt had told them to do;

they let the boys live. "

(Exodus 1:17, CEB)

Because Shiprah and Puah 'feared God,' they made the courageous decision to continue delivering babies as always. Defying Pharaoh's order was dangerous, and they were inevitably called before the throne to explain why the baby boys were still alive. They took another risky step — they lied.

Then the king of Egypt summoned the

midwives and asked them, "Why have you done this?

Why have you let the boys live? "

The midwives answered Pharaoh, "Hebrew

women are not like Egyptian women; they are

vigorous and give birth before the midwives arrive. "

(Exodus 1:18-19, CEB)

The women's legs must have been shaking as they stood before

Pharaoh's throne, chins held high as they fed him their tall tale. *Would he*

see through their story and order them to prison or even death?

But God was with them. Pharaoh shooed them away and we are

told that God was "kind" to them and gave them families of their own.

For a time, the baby boys were allowed to thrive.

Adam Hamilton points out in his book *Moses: In the Footsteps of*

the Reluctant Prophet, that while we do not know the name of the Pharaoh

in the story, Shiprah and Puah's names are known and celebrated 3,300

years later.[1]

What can we learn from these brave women about standing up for

our own beliefs, even when it means defying or disobeying the law?

1. We need to go on our knees first and pray for clarity.

Watching the evening news is enough to get me riled up in anger.

But does my righteous anger come because I see true injustice, or because

others are acting in ways I disagree with? Do the actions of others go

against the Bible or against my personal prejudices?

The first thing we need to do when faced with something we feel is unethical or against our Christian beliefs is to go on our knees and ask God for guidance. The midwives' reason for disobeying Pharaoh was because "they feared God." They may have had other reasons, but their belief that it was wrong in God's eyes was their primary motivator.

We need to make sure our motives are pure and in line with Biblical teachings before we act. In his Sermon on the Mount, Jesus tells us over and over to approach evil people with love, not hate.

"You have heard that it was said, You must love your

neighbor and hate your enemy. But I say to you, love

your enemies and pray for those who harass you

so that you will be acting as children of your

Father who is in heaven.

(Matthew 5:43-45a, CEB)

What emotion is paramount in my heart? When I find myself responding with anger toward someone, I need to examine my own heart.

2. We need to ask God to guide our actions.

The midwives prayed for the best way to keep Pharaoh from killing the baby boys. They had a plan and stayed united behind it. Without calling attention to their rebuff of Pharaoh's command, they quietly continued doing their work of bringing babies into the world.

Scripture tells us in Ecclesiastes that there is "a time to be silent and a time to speak" (Ecclesiastes 3 :7). Sometimes we need to march and be vocal about what we believe, and other times we need to work for justice through our vote, our money, or through helping someone on a personal level. The most loving response may be to pray for those that offend us and make the effort to have a conversation with them.

When we feel that we are not equipped for the task of standing up for our beliefs, we need to remember that we have been given the given the "ministry of reconciliation":

"All of these new things are from God, who reconciled us to himself through Christ and who gave us the ministry of reconciliation... We are therefore

Christ's ambassadors, as though God were making

his appeal through us. We implore you on Christ's

behalf: Be reconciled to God."

(II Corinthians 5:18, 20, NIV)

I often fall into the trap of thinking that important reconciliation efforts are left up to the professional diplomats or counselors. But this verse brings home the powerful realization that God has called *me* to be his ambassador — his representative in the world. I have the responsibility of bringing together all people to find reconciliation through Christ.

Are we bringing about reconciliation or division by our actions? Sometimes, as in the case of Shiprah and Puah, division is necessary, but we need to approach these situations prayerfully.

3. We need to remember that although we may feel that our efforts are inconsequential, they can have a lasting impact.

No action that we take to stand up for our beliefs is ever wasted. Shiprah and Puah were not military leaders or important to Pharaoh, but they did their small part to make a difference.

Pharaoh continued to kill the babies, but the midwives' courage allowed one mother to be able to hide her son for three months. This mother put her baby in a reed basket and placed him in the Nile, hoping that Pharaoh's daughter would find him and allow him to live.

God's plan was fulfilled through that baby, who was pulled from the river and named Moses by Pharaoh's daughter. He would ultimately lead his people out of bondage in Egypt.

At times I feel like the disciple Andrew, when Jesus told him to feed a huge crowd of people with the offering of one little boy's lunch:

"A youth here has five barley loaves and two fish.

But what good is that for a crowd like this?"

(John 6:9, CEB)

Surely my little bit cannot make a difference. But all of us working together in small ways can cause a wave of change. We may never know how an act of defiance against prejudice or immorality may change the thoughts and feelings of someone else.

Prayer: Dear God, thank you for all those who have gone before me with the courage to stand up for what they believed. Give me the sensitivity, insight, and boldness to step out on faith to protest injustice and immorality in whatever way you call me. Amen.

Questions to ponder:

When have I let fear hold me back from standing up for what I believe? Is there a situation right now that I can change in some small way by writing a letter, sending an email, or donating money? Is God calling me to protest an injustice in a more active way?

Is there someone in your life who is causing anger in your life right now? Bring that person before the Lord in prayer. Ask him to lead you to take the first steps toward reconciliation.

Footnotes:

1. Hamilton, A. (2017). *Moses: In the footsteps of the reluctant prophet*. Abingdon Press.